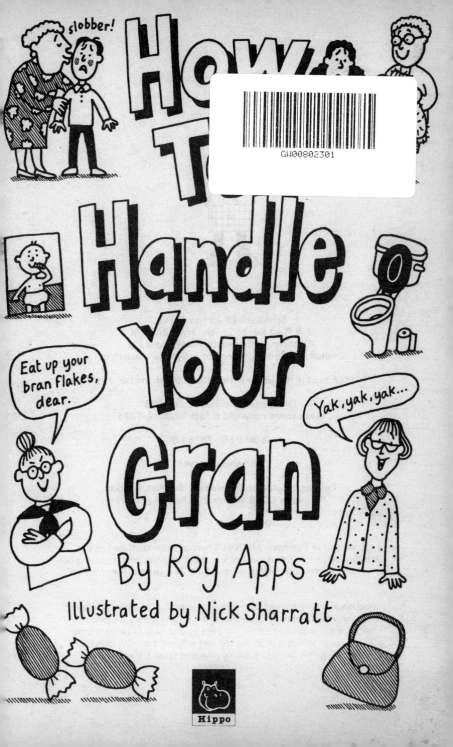

Scholastic Children's Books,
7-9 Pratt Street, London NW1 0AE, UK
A division of Scholastic Publications Ltd
London ~ New York ~ Toronto ~ Sydney ~ Auckland

Published in the UK by Scholastic Publications Ltd, 1995

Text copyright © Roy Apps, 1995
Illustrations copyright © Nick Sharratt, 1995

ISBN 0 590 13150 8

Typeset by Contour Typesetters, Southall, London
Printed by Cox & Wyman Ltd, Reading, Berks

10 9 8 7 6

!!! Warning !!!

The book that you are now reading contains highly explosive material!

The reason for this is:

1 It's a very *handy* book.
2 It's an *aid* to help you cope with your *gran*.
3 In other words, it's –

A HAND-Y GRAN-AID!

Because this book is so dangerous, once you have finished with it, you are strongly advised to place it carefully in a paper bag and blow it up.

This won't destroy it, but it will make a really good noise.

Contents

How this book all started – the letter from my gran

It all started one fine morning, a few months ago. I got up, went to the bathroom and cleaned my teeth. I slipped on something casual – my tee-shirt and jeans. Then I slipped on something pink and slithery – a bar of soap.

Half a second later I was at the foot of the stairs. I looked up and saw that there were seven letters on the front door mat. I read them quickly and this is what they said:

ƎWOƆ˥ƎM

Then I saw that there was another letter on the door mat. I opened it . . .

Flat 80 The Old Granary
75 Gran Parade
Nantwich
NA1 NA2

My dear grandson

. . . it began. I wondered who could be writing to me in such a manner. After some thought, I decided it had to be one of two people: either my gran – or my other gran. I read some more . . .

!!! Another Warning !!!

THIS BIT IS REALLY GRISLY AND GRUESOME. IF YOU ARE OF A PARTICULARLY SENSITIVE NATURE, EITHER SKIP IT OR READ IT WITH YOUR EYES SHUT. THE PUBLISHERS WILL BEAR NO RESPONSIBILITY FOR ANY ILL-EFFECTS YOU MIGHT SUFFER AFTER READING IT.

It seems like only yesterday that you were the cutest of little chappies, always ready with a cuddle for your darling gran, and always happy to give me a big kiss whenever I had to say, "Bye bye, my darling liddle boy!"

THERE!
DON'T SAY YOU
WEREN'T WARNED!

If you feel a bit icky-sicky after reading that, then pop to the bathroom NOW!

Better?

Good.

Because there's more.

What went wrong, my pet? Why couldn't gran's special boy have done something worthwhile with his life, like studying brain surgery or becoming a contestant on Strike it Lucky? Why did you have to go and write a book telling people how to handle their mums?* Oh, the shame of it!

Called How to Handle Your Mum *and published by Hippo Books at only £2.50! Great value! In all good bookshops now! And in quite a few bad ones too!*

> I enclose a handbill that was pushed through my letter box.* It seems that, encouraged by you, some people have now set themselves up as experts on grandmothers.

. . . the letter ran.

So I ran after it.

Come back here!

When I caught it up, I saw that this was how it ended . . .

* See p. 13.

Well, let me tell you this, young man – don't you ever dare write a book telling people how to handle their grans. Because, if you do, I shall never, ever knit you another maroon zip-up cardigan for your birthday or Christmas present again.

Your ever doting
Gran

P.S. <u>NOT</u> YOUR <u>OTHER</u> GRAN

If the picture of me sitting around in a maroon zip-up cardigan brings tears to your eyes, don't worry.

Turn over and wipe your eyes on the back of the page.
(Don't sneeze into it, though. Otherwise, it won't be a tissue, but *atishoo*!)

This was the handbill that was pushed
through my gran's door:

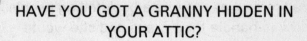

HAVE YOU GOT A GRANNY HIDDEN IN
YOUR ATTIC?

HAVE YOU GOT A GRAN WHO'S BEEN IN
YOUR FAMILY FOR YEARS?

WOULD YOU LIKE TO KNOW HOW OLD SHE
IS?

WOULD YOU LIKE TO KNOW HOW
VALUABLE SHE IS?

YES? THEN BRING HER ALONG TO:

THE GRANTIQUES ROADSHOW

FOR AN EXPERT OPINION AND FREE
ADVICE

PLUS !!!!!!

ALL GRANNY-RELATED OBJECTS BROUGHT
ALONG WILL BE SCIENTIFICALLY TESTED

Of course, there was only one thing I could do after getting a letter like that from my gran. I'd been trying to stop her knitting me maroon zip-up cardigans for ages. Now all I had to do was to write a book telling people how to handle their grans and she would never send me another maroon zip-up cardigan again!

I rushed upstairs to my word-processor. I knew what to write. For, although Gran didn't know it, one of the experts on *The Grantiques Roadshow* was me! I switched on my word-processor and began to type at speed. I wrote:

HOO PO HODDLE YUIR GRUN

I thought I might just possibly have made one or two typing errors, so I ran it through the Spell Check. Then it read . . .

COW POO HUDDLE YOUR GRIN

I was almost there!

How To Handle Your Gran: Stage One

Learning how to date your gran

Now you might think that grans are just like antiques; that is, they are all old. This would be a dreadful mistake. For while it is true that *some* grans are old, not all of them are. For example, some of them are *ancient*, while others are simply *prehistoric*.

Dating *antiques* is easy-peasy. Dating grans is very difficult indeed. A *Grantiques Roadshow* expert spent years devising a way of dating grans.

His first thought was:

Why don't we count their teeth like you do to find out how old a horse is!

So he asked a passing gran:

"Excuse me for asking, but how many teeth have you got?"

The gran gave him a thumping good reply. With her handbag. Result: The gran had forty teeth. All of them belonging to the expert.

The *Grantiques Roadshow* expert's second thought was:

*Doesh anyone know
a good dentisht?*

Then the expert thought:

*You can tell the age
of a tree by the
number of rings it has.
Why don't we do the
same with grans?*

So he asked a passing gran:

"Excuse me for asking, but can you tell me how many rings you've got under your eyes?"

The gran saw red. And so did the expert. He also saw green, violet, orange, blue and mauve.

While he was recovering in hospital, the expert at last devised a safe and foolproof method of finding out – roughly – how old your gran is.

However, the details are so secret that the expert who discovered this winning formula absolutely forbade me to print it here.

So I decided to print it here instead.

TEST YOURSELF!!! with the *Grantiques Roadshow* gran "dating" procedure

Ask your gran the following question:
   "Do you remember the Queen's coronation, gran?"

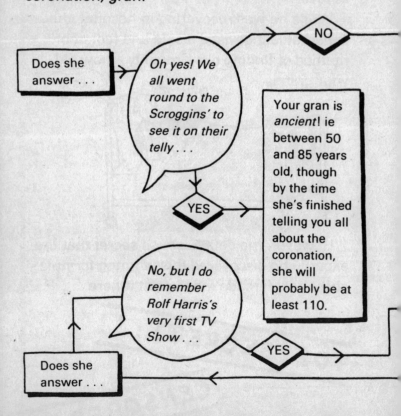

Does she answer . . .

Oh yes! We all went round to the Scroggins' to see it on their telly . . .

NO

YES

Your gran is *ancient*! ie between 50 and 85 years old, though by the time she's finished telling you all about the coronation, she will probably be at least 110.

No, but I do remember Rolf Harris's very first TV Show . . .

Does she answer . . .

YES

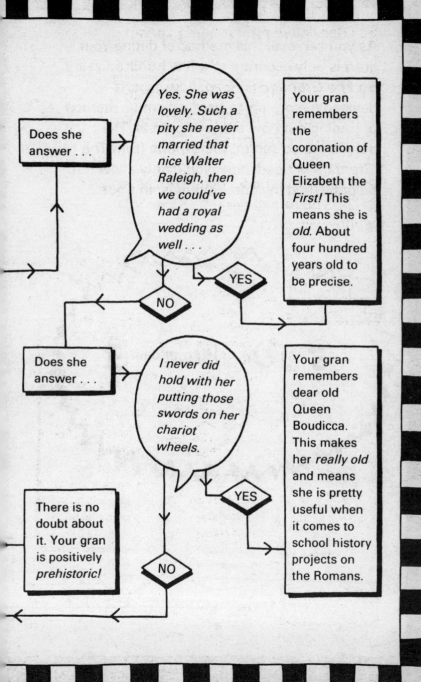

As you can see, this method of dating your gran is only accurate to a few hundred years. So *The Grantiques Roadshow* experts devised a more up-to-date, scientific method of finding out how old your gran is. The details are so secret, the experts from *The Grantiques Roadshow* would only allow it to be published in code. Here it is. In Code.

C Ask O your D grandad! E

How To Handle Your Gran: Stage Two

Learning to recognize the difference between antiques and grantiques

In some ways, grans *are* like antiques. That is, they are very valuable. However, antiques are valuable because they are old. Grans are valuable because they:

1 Are good cooks (most of the time)

2 Can be generous with pocket money

3 Can take you on good outings

4 Can tell really wicked stories about your mum or dad – like the time your mum ran away from home when she was five, or the time your dad scored four own goals for the school football team. Chortle chortle!

So, you can see, there will be many differences between an expert on *antiques* and an expert on *grantiques*.

For example, an expert from *The **Antiques** Roadshow* will be able to spot the difference between a Chippendale chair (made by the famous English furniture designer, T. Chippendale) and a Fake chair (made by the infamous English furniture designer, A. Fake).

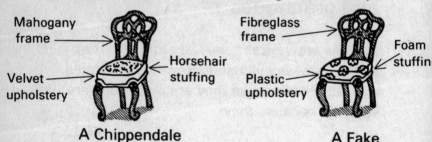

Mahogany frame → ← Horsehair stuffing
Velvet upholstery →

Fibreglass frame → Foam stuffin
Plastic upholstery →

A Chippendale

A Fake

On the other hand, an expert from *The **Grantiques** Roadshow* will be able to spot the difference between a Chippendale and a granny.

A Chippendale

A Granny

And another thing. An expert from *The Antiques Roadshow* would say . . .

"What an exquisite chair! Notice the knobbly legs and the padded seat . . ."

Whereas an expert on grantiques would say . . .

"What an exquisite gran! Notice the knobbly knees and the padded seat . . ."

And while this might very well be *true*, it wouldn't actually tell us very much about *how to handle* her. For although your gran is valuable (see page 21), she is likely to be rather like a nun with no dress sense. That is, she'll have some absolutely dreadful habits.

She will therefore need careful *handling* if you are to get the best out of her. To do that, it is vital that you find out just what kind of gran (or grans) you have got, because different types of gran have different dreadful habits.

TEST YOURSELF!!! on the difference between grantiques and antiques

In each of the boxes below is a statement about an *antique* and a statement about a *grantique*. Can you match the statement with grantique or antique?

Which one of these is:
1 very *easy* to wind up
and which is:
2 very *difficult* to wind up?

a a rusty antique clock   b your gran

Which one of these is:
3 *a little pot*
and which is:
4 *a little potty*?

Half past eight - time for beddy-byes.

c your gran's views on staying up late   d a small antique vase

Which one of these opens to reveal:
5 a dreadful *pong*
and which opens to reveal:
6 a dreadful *prong*?

e your gran's make-up   f an antique
   bag   Swiss Army knife

Which one of these is:
7 wearing a *little fin* on top
and which is:
8 wearing a *little thin* on top?

g an antique stuffed   h your gran's
   goldfish   hairdo

Which one of these shows evidence of:
9 *wet rot*
and which shows evidence of:
10 Wet Wet Wet *rot*?

i your gran's views   j an antique
   on music   wardrobe that's been
                               left out in the rain

Answers 1 = b; 2 = a; 3 = d; 4 = c; 5 = e;
6 = f; 7 = g; 8 = h; 9 = j; 10 = i.

How To Handle Your Gran: Stage Three

Learning to recognize what type of gran you've got, and how to handle them

During my years working for *The Grantiques Roadshow*, I identified three main granny types:

GRANNY
– a big granny type

GRANNY
– a fancy granny type

GRANNY
– a faint granny type

COLLAPSE!

Not only that, but the grans people brought along to *The Grantiques Roadshow* fell into five types, each with their own annoying habits:

Gran type No. 1: The Telly-gran
This perfect example of a *telly-gran* was brought to me at *The Grantiques Roadshow* by Jodie Brodie.

GLAD-IAT-ORS!

Telly-grans are not very interesting, I'm afraid. Being telly-grans means that they're always watching television. A telly-gran's favourite TV programme is *Gladiators*. This reminds her of the good old days when your grandad used to take her to watch Millwall on a Saturday afternoon. Of course, if *Gladiators* isn't on, they'll watch anything on *Gran*ada.

So, do you think you've got a telly-gran? Your answers to the checklist question will reveal all . . .

Stage 3 first check!!!

The following question has been designed by *Grantiques Roadshow* experts to tell you whether you've got a telly-gran or not.

Which of the following things does your gran wear?

(a) Lots of perfume   YES/NO
(b) Rubber boots   YES/NO
(c) A little grey beard on her chin   YES/NO
(d) Orange and lime green beach shorts and a vacant expression on her face   YES/NO

What the answers mean:

(a) If you've answered YES, don't worry. The chances are your gran's not a telly-gran, but a *smelly*-gran.

(b) If you've answered YES, don't worry. Your gran's not a telly-gran, but a *welly*-gran.

(c) If you've answered YES, then your name's Darren Dipstick. (see p. 53.)

(d) If you've answered YES to this one, then hard luck. Your gran's such a fine example of a telly-gran that she already thinks she's a character in an Australian soap.

Fair dinkum, sport!

If you answered YES to (d), *don't panic*! Just shove your telly-gran back in front of the telly until you've finished the next four pages, which are going to give you some tips on handling telly-grans.

The good news about telly-grans is . . .

1 They leave you alone.
2 That's it.

The bad news about telly-grans is . . .

1 If you ask them anything, they'll just go into puncture mode: that is, they'll go:

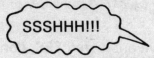

SSSHHH!!!

They are, I'm afraid, completely worthless, because you can never get anything of any value out of them. Jodie Brodie demonstrated this sad fact to me at *The Grantiques Roadshow*.

JODIE: Gran? Could I have an ice-cream please?
TELLY-GRAN: Ssshhh!!!!

And again . . .

JODIE: Gran? Would you tell me about how naughty Dad was when he was a boy?
TELLY-GRAN: Ssshhh!!!!

You can stand on your head in front of a telly-gran, blowing raspberries and juggling half a dozen eggs with your feet, and all she'll say is:

"You're blocking my view of the screen, dear."

So how can you give a telly-gran some value? In other words, get some money out of her for – say – a Six-Flavour-Double-Whopper-With-Extra-Flake (i.e. your favourite ice-cream)?

Handling Telly-grans the *Grantiques Roadshow* way

The Bike Shop Solution

First of all, put up the sign that's on the next page on your front door.

Remember to write your name on the dots. I don't mean actually write "YOUR NAME". I mean write "C. Lyon" or "Oz Stritch" or "Ellie Fant" or whatever your mum and dad decided to call you when you were born.

When everyone starts arriving with their bikes, you take them into the sitting room. You say:

"Gran? Could I have a Six-Flavour-Double-Whopper-With-Extra-Flake please?"

And as soon as she says

"Ssshhh!!!!"

You shove the valve up to her mouth so she blows it up with her *"Ssshhh!!!!"*-ing. She won't notice, because she'll be too busy watching telly.

Soon you'll have so many 10p's you'll be able to buy enough Six-Flavour-Double-Whoppers-With-Extra-Flakes to build an edible igloo.

The disadvantage of this solution

It is very difficult to stop telly-grans going *"Ssshhh!!!!"* once they've started, so you could end up with a sitting room full of exploding tyres.

Gran type No. 2: The Bran Gran

Herbert McSherbet brought his bran gran along to *The Grantiques Roadshow* last summer. He was staying with her on holiday. Bran grans tend to be the sort of gran you stay with on holiday.

Bran grans are quite a curiosity really: they're always worried that you haven't been going to the toilet regularly. When you're out with them, they're always asking you: "Are you sure you don't need to go to the loo?"

Think you've got a bran gran? Your answers to the checklist question will reveal all . . .

Stage 3 second check!!!

The following question has been designed by *Grantiques Roadshow* experts to tell you whether you've got a bran gran or not.

What is your gran's favourite food? Is it . . .

(a) Bran flakes and prunes   YES/NO
(b) Bran cakes and prunes   YES/NO
(c) Bran bakes and prunes   YES/NO
(d) Cheese and bunion crisps   YES/NO

What the answers mean:

(a) (b) and (c) If you've answered YES, hard cheese, you've got a bran gran.

(d) If you've answered YES, hard bran, you've got a cheese gran. Count yourself lucky. Cheese and bunion crisps taste a lot better than bran flakes.

The good news about bran grans is . . .

1 They've always got plenty of food in the fridge.

The bad news about bran grans is . . .

1 The sort of food that they've got in the fridge. (See (a), (b) and (c) above.)

Instead of giving you a nice bowl of Golden Grahams for breakfast, bran grans will try to make you eat:

1 Prunes.
2 "210% Bran Flakes" which look like something that has come out of the end of a pencil sharpener – and which taste like it too.

A typical conversation with a bran gran will go:

BRAN GRAN: What a lovely morning. I thought we'd make up a picnic and go somewhere nice.
YOU: Great! Where are we going?
BRAN GRAN: Have you been to *the toilet?*
YOU: (Stunned silence, thinking . . . *Why are we going to have a picnic in the toilet?*)

Bran grans are quite valuable grantiques, though. Because, if you ever go out with them, they always give you 20p ("Just in case you need the Superloo, dear.") Also, they're particularly handy if you're a keen train-spotter, because they're always happy to take you to Waterloo.

The real problem, though, is how to avoid all the bran flake and prune breakfasts when you're staying with them. There are two possible solutions:

Handling Bran grans the *Grantiques Roadshow* way

1 The Runaway Chain Solution

When you first arrive at your gran's, head straight for the bathroom. It is handy to have a bundle of *Batman* or *Fast Forward* magazines and a length of string.

Get yourself comfortable on the bathroom floor with your magazines.

Tie one end of the piece of string around your big toe and the other end around the handle on the loo. Keep pulling at regular intervals. When you have finished all your comics, come out. Your gran will look at you with great concern and say:

"Dear me, I don't think you'll *be needing any bran flakes and prunes for breakfast!"*

The disadvantage of this solution

It only works for a couple of days. After that, your bran gran starts to get suspicious. Not only that, you'll have read all your comics twice and they'll be getting really boring.

The other solution is:

2 The Mad Grandchild Disease solution

This involves getting someone really big to deal with the situation. I don't mean someone-big-like-the-class-heavies Barry Beefcake and Belinda Bludgeon. I mean someone-big-like-important. I mean *the Prime Minister*. All you need to do is to get him to send your gran a letter warning her about the dreadful dangers of eating prunes and bran flakes. Simple, eh?

There are two ways of carrying out the Mad Grandchild Disease solution. Either you can ring up the Prime Minister and ask him to send your gran the letter straight away, or, if you haven't got his phone number handy, you can use the letter on the next page . . .

H M GOVERNMENT

The Prime Minister
10 Downing Street
London SW1

Dear Mrs . . . . . .

Whatever you do, don't give your grandchild
. . . . . . any prunes or bran flakes for breakfast.
    According to recent research, they could
give . . . . . . Mad Grandchild Disease, or MGD
as it's known in the trade.
    The effects of MGD include the patient
becoming extremely noisy with a tendency to
dance on the furniture and, worst of all, sing
the greatest hits of *Take That* at the top of his
or her voice. Pretty dreadful, I think you'll
agree.
    My advice is to give your grandchild a
really scrummy breakfast, e.g. eggs, bacon,
tomatoes, sausages and fries, waffles with
maple syrup, even Golden Grahams, all
washed down with a couple of strawberry
milk-shakes.
    Must dash now, as Noddy's on the telly in
a minute.

Yours sincerely

The Prime Minister

Don't forget to write your name on the dotted line, and your gran's name after the "Dear Mrs". Then leave the letter on the doormat for your gran to collect with the morning post.

The disadvantage of this solution

. . . is this. After your gran's read the letter from the Prime Minister, her conversation with you could go something like this . . .

YOUR GRAN: Something smells a bit fishy here.
YOU: (Playing it well cool) Oh good. Are we having kippers for breakfast?
YOUR GRAN: I meant . . . I can smell a rat!
YOU: We're not having *rat* for breakfast, are we? I think I'd prefer prunes and bran flakes, although it would be a pretty close run thing –
YOUR GRAN: I'm talking about this letter from the Prime Minister. I think it's a fake!
YOU: (Gulp) Why, Gran?
YOUR GRAN: For a start, I can understand every word he's saying! But not only that . . . I turned the letter over and do you know what I found on the back of it?
YOU: No . . .
YOUR GRAN: This conversation!

(*She's right, of course.*)

YOUR GRAN: Of course I'm right!

Gran type No. 3: The Kisser-gran

Kisser-grans are really quite common. The chances are you have at least one. I came across this grisly and gruesome example of a kisser-gran at *The Grantiques Roadshow* earlier in the year.

slobber!

Think you've got a kisser-gran or two? Your answers to the checklist question will tell you . . .

Stage 3 Third check!!!

The following question has been designed by *Grantiques Roadshow* experts to tell you whether you've got a kisser-gran or not.

Where does your gran kiss you? Is it . . .

(a) On your right cheek   YES/NO
(b) On your left cheek   YES/NO
(c) On the end of your nose   YES/NO
(d) On your neck   YES/NO
(e) All of these   YES/NO

What the answers mean:

(a) and (b) If you've answered YES, then I'm afraid you've got a kisser-gran.

(c) If you've answered YES, then your gran needs glasses.

(d) If you've answered YES, then your gran thinks she's a vampire.

(e) If you've answered YES, then you've got a short-sighted kisser-gran who thinks she's a vampire.

The good news about kisser-grans is . . .

1 They like giving you things: sweets, pocket
money, outings . . .

The bad news about kisser-grans is . . .

1 The things they like giving you most of all
are sloppy, slobbery *kisses*.
2 Yuk.

Kisser·grans are rather like tubes of
super glue. That is, you get stuck with them.
If you try to get away from them, something
like this is bound to happen . . .

YOU: Bye then, Gran. I've got to go.
KISSER-GRAN: Must you, dear?
YOU: Yes. I'm taking part in the first ever
World Slug-Racing Championships round at
Wayne Payne's.
KISSER-GRAN: Ohhh . . . how about a big
kiss for your gran before you go then . . .?

RESULT: you get kissed. It's exactly like
having your pet slug Arnold crawl across
your cheek, and it puts you off slug racing for
the rest of your life.

Handling kisser-grans the *Grantiques Roadshow* way

The Pong Solution

If you've got older brothers or boy cousins, you will have noticed that once they get to about thirteen, they aren't bothered by kisser-grans. You probably wonder how they manage this. I can give you the answer in one word.

Pong.

Or to give it its scientific name: After-shave Lotion.

You may have thought that the reason your older brother/cousin and all your friends' older brothers tip bottles of after-shave lotion over their faces was to try and impress Sharon Shaddock (the Year 9 disco-dancing champion), but you'd be wrong. The reason your older brother and your friends' older brothers all tip bottles of after-shave over their faces is to ward off kisser-grans.

If you don't believe me, just sneak into your older brother's bedroom and have a sniff of his after-shave lotion. Poooohhhh!!! What a pong! If you were Sharon Shaddock, would *that* make you feel all lovey-dovey? Of course not. It would be more likely to make you feel all icky-sicky. No wonder kisser-grans keep well clear of it.

The problem is that really pongy after-shave lotion costs a lot of money. However, help is at hand, or rather *in* your hand, because *The Grantiques Roadshow* experts have devised a recipe for home-made after-shave lotion in nine and a half easy steps:

The *Grantiques Roadshow* recipe for

PONG

1 Put a peg on your nose.
2 Take six rotten Brussels sprouts* and a few rotten cabbage leaves.
3 Mash them up together.
4 Add half a cup of slime juice and half a tablespoon of the cheesy bits from between your toes.
5. Mash some more.
6. Add a pinch of squashed snail,** and two heaped tablespoons of strong black pepper.
7 Mash some more.
8 Allow to marinate overnight.
9 Apply liberally to both cheeks next time your gran comes.
9½ Keep the peg on your nose.

There. I think you'll agree it's a recipe not to be sneezed at. Or rather it is.

* The round green sort; not the sort that wear scarves and woggles.
** If you haven't got any squashed snails, Pot Noodle will do.

The disadvantages of this solution

1 Having to wear a peg on your nose means you'll end up talking through door dode dike dis.
2 If you've got an older brother, he'll try and nick it to use as after-shave lotion, before you get a chance to try it out on your kisser-gran.

Gran type No. 4: The Grow-nan

Here is Kylie Riley's grow-nan.

Kylie sees her grow-nan every week. And each time, the first thing her grow-nan says to her is:
   *"My goodness! You have **grown** since I last saw you!!!"**
   The second thing she says is:
   *"My goodness! You have **grown** since I last saw you!!!"***

* *i.e. three days ago.*
** *i.e. three seconds ago.*

And that's another reason they're called grow-nans: everything thay say makes you groan.

Does this all sound horribly familiar? "YES" answers to the checklist question will confirm the worst . . .

Stage 3 fourth check!!!

The following question has been designed by *Grantiques Roadshow* experts to tell you whether your gran's a grow-nan or not.

Where does your gran think you go to school? Is it . . .

(a) The playgroup in the church hall   YES/NO

(b) The playgroup in the scout hut   YES/NO

(c) Grange Hill comprehensive
    YES/NO

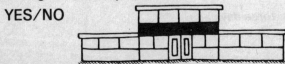

What the answers mean:

(a) and (b) If you've answered YES, then ahhhh! Coo-chee coo-chee coo! You've got a grow-nan.

(c) If you've answered YES, then you've got a telly-gran. (But you probably knew that already.)

The good news about grow-nans is . . .

1 As they still think you go to playgroup, they're not likely to turn up at your school.
2 There is a steady second-hand trade in grow-nans. For example, the TV personalities Ronnie Corbett and Paul Daniels have both bought grow-nans at grantique shops recently. This is so that when they come down to breakfast each morning, there is someone sitting there to tell them:

*"My goodness, Ronald/Paul! You have grown since I last saw you!!!"**

* *This is completely untrue, of course.*

The bad news about grow-nans is . . .

1 They can't help thinking that you are still a baby.* For example, Kylie Riley's gran bought her a large shiny ring for her birthday. Now you might think that a large shiny ring would be just tickateeboo for a smart girl like Kylie. But, of course, Kylie's gran was a grow-nan. The ring she bought her looked like this:

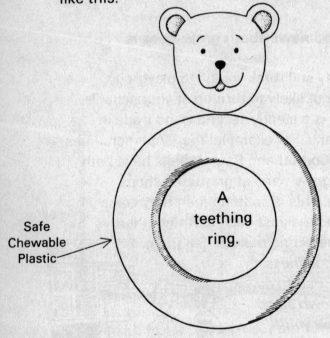

Safe Chewable Plastic

A teething ring.

* *This is why the most famous grow-nan of them all (who has had a number of gruesome films made about her) is called Grow-nan the Baby-arian.*

Handling grow-nans the *Grantiques Roadshow* way

The shock tactic

The only way to make a grow-nan see sense is to give her a big shock. There are two methods of doing this. Unfortunately, if you use the first method, you are likely to fuse all the lights in the house. The second method is even more dangerous. First, learn the following words from *The Grantiques Roadshow Phrasebook.*

YO	MAN
COOL	GIMME
	YEE-AH
HANGIN'	
HEY	BIN
DUDE	

Then next time your grow-nan calls, make sure you're wearing a decent pair of shades and the conversation should go something like this:

GRAN: My good –
YOU: (*Interrupting her*) Yee-Ah!!! Hey gran!!!
Hey!!! Where you bin hangin' out, man?
GRAN: – ness –

(*Come on! Quickly, before she can say
"You have grown since I last saw you!"*)

YOU: – Yo gran, you cool dude! Hey, gimme
one!

(*Go on! Slap her palms.*)

GRAN: (*Too shocked to reply*)

You may be cool, but your gran is now like a
Sainsbury's turkey, i.e. frozen. To the spot.
Because she is in deep shock.

You see, up until now your grow-nan has
always thought of you as a little mite with a
pretty face and the vocabulary of a talking
dolly. Now she has seen you as a big fright
with a twitty face and the vocabulary of a

talking wally. She will never look at you in the same light again. Particularly if you let her wear your shades.

Gran type No. 5: The Nanny

The fifth sort of gran brought to the *Grantiques Roadshow* was Darren Dipstick's nanny. She was very fidgety. She had white hair, bulging eyes and a small beard on her chin. I took a long look at her. Then I took a short look at her and asked Darren this question . . .

ME: Why have you brought me your pet goat?

Well, what else can you expect from Darren Dipstick? He's just a kid.

TEST YOURSELF!!! on types of grans

1 Which of the following are types of grans?

   a Telly-grans?
   b Telly Venables?
   c Bran grans?
   d Bran tubs?
   e Kisser-grans?
   f A hoover?
   g Grow-nans?
   h Grow-bags?
   i Darren Dipstick's nanny?

2 Which of the following is the best way to handle a telly-gran?

   a Stand on your head blowing raspberries and juggling half a dozen eggs with your feet?

   b Stand on your little brother's head blowing raspberries and juggling half a dozen eggs with your feet?
   c Set up a bike shop?

3 Who is most likely to help you handle a bran gran?

   a The Terminator?

   b The Prime Minister?

   c Mr Blobby?

4 Which of the following is likely to help you handle a kisser-gran?

   a A few rotten cabbage leaves?

   b Half a cup of slime juice?

   c Half a tablespoon of the cheesy bits from between your toes?

5 Why would a grow-nan be frozen to the spot?

   a Because she's standing in a bucket of ice cubes?

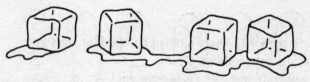

   b Because she's mistaken the freezer for the toilet?

   c Because you've said, "Yo gran, you cool dude! Hey, gimme one!"

Answers

1 a; c; e and g are right: score 1 point for each. Also score three-quarters of a point for f (hoovers). Being kissed by a gran is very similar to putting the nozzle of a hoover to your cheek and turning it on full power.

2 a No points. You're cracked! And so, no doubt, are the eggs.

b No points. You're cracked! And so, no doubt, are the eggs and your little brother's head.

c 1 point.

3 a Minus 20 points. You must be joking! The Terminator would be scared stiff by your gran.

b 1 point.

c Three-quarters of a point. (It *is* easy to confuse Mr Blobby with the Prime Minister.)

4 1 point for a, b and c. If you put all three, you're probably thinking you smell success. You don't. You smell awful.

5 a No points. You've just got a very nervous gran, i.e. she's got cold feet.

b No points. In fact, put this book down and go and let her out immediately!

c 1 point.

Your score

More than 12? There's only one word for somebody with a score like that. Cheat.

Between 3 and 12? Yo, gimme one! (As you might say to a grow-nan.) Now proceed to Stage 4.

Less than 3? You're obviously the one who's been standing on their head, blowing raspberries and juggling half a dozen eggs with their feet. Now go and sit down and read this section again properly.

How To Handle Your Gran: Stage Four

Learning to handle your gran's five deadly grantique weapons

Your gran may *look* like a sweet little old lady, but underneath she's as hard as nails.* Ever wondered why she carries such a big handbag? It contains five secret grantique weapons for dealing with the likes of you.

These deadly weapons were first used by one of the most famous of all grannies, the Granny Secret Agent, 0070 Granny Bond – licensed to knit. This is how it was described in the well-known Granny Bond story, *Oldfinger* . . .

*If you don't know how hard nails are, try testing a couple from the pile under your bed – especially the big toe ones.

Granny Bond straightened her perm and marched into Q.T's office. Q.T. was the phenomenally brilliant scientist and inventor who made all of Granny Bond's special secret weapons. He was called Q.T. because Granny Bond was always calling him "cutie".

"How's my little cutie?" asked Granny Bond, planting a really slobbery kiss on his chin. Yes, as you may have guessed, Granny Bond was a kisser-gran.*

"Can I get you a drink?" asked Q.T.

"Yes, please. A cup of tea would go down very well. You know how I like it?"

"Strong, with a dash of milk: shaken not stirred."

As Granny Bond sipped her tea, Q.T. explained the plan.

* See pages 41 to 47.

"Too many grandchildren are getting their own way with their grans. That's why I have designed a blueprint for a special handbag containing five grantique weapons. Each of these weapons is especially designed to act on one of a grandson's or granddaughter's five senses."

With a flourish Q.T. produced a detailed diagram.

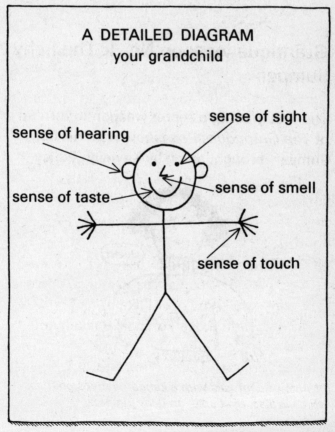

A DETAILED DIAGRAM
your grandchild

sense of sight

sense of hearing

sense of smell

sense of taste

sense of touch

"Make sure you never set out on a mission to your grandchildren without this handbag of weapons," added Q.T.

Since then, all of Granny Bond's secret weapons have turned up at *The Grantiques Roadshow*, and grantiques experts have developed ways of dealing with them and turning them to your advantage.

Grantique weapon No. 1: The Itchy Jumper

The first grantique secret weapon to turn up at *The Grantiques Roadshow* was this Itchy Jumper* brought along by Kayleigh Bailey.

* Not to be confused with a kangaroo that's got fleas, which is also, of course, an itchy jumper.

As you can see, this grantique weapon is not so much a weapon of war as a weapon of *wear*. Here are some facts:

The *Grantiques Roadshow* Grantique Weapons Factsheet No. 1

THE ITCHY JUMPER

Designed to act on: Your sense of touch.

What your gran says when she sees you wearing it: "What a really amazing knit!"

What your friends say when they see you wearing it: "What a really amazing nit!"

Feels like: You're wearing a giant brillo pad.

Most in use: At Christmas and birthdays.

"That's all very interesting."
. . . said Kayleigh Bailey.
"But how do I get rid
of it?"

To which I replied, "Do
what Theseus did."

"And who was he when he
was at home?"

"I'm just about
to tell you."

"Thank you."

Theseus was an ancient Greek. And being an ancient Greek, he had an ancient gran. This ancient gran knitted him a truly awful itchy jumper. His mates all laughed at him and said, "What a really amazing nit!"* So Theseus decided that it had to be got rid of.

One fine day, he said to his gran, "I think I'll go and slay the dreadful monster known as the Minotaur, that lives in the creepy caves by yonder cliffs."

His gran said, "Well, don't be late for tea." And she gave Theseus a big kiss on the cheek because she was a kisser-gran.**

When Theseus got to the entrance to the Minotaur's creepy cave, he wondered how he would ever manage to find his way out again.

"Ouch!" he yelled, rubbing his head. For something had struck him. It was a thought.

* See p. 62 above
** See p. 41 above.

"If I tie the end of my itchy jumper round
this spike, it'll unravel as I go and I'll be able
to find my way back by it!" he declared.

By the time he reached the Minotaur's lair,
he was only wearing half an itchy jumper.
Even so, it was such a dreadful sight, the
Minotaur roared –

"Ooooo!!!! Help! Mummy!"

Then it ran off and was never seen again.

By the time Theseus had followed the trail
of wool back to the entrance of the cave, the
other half of his jumper had unravelled.

"Hurrah! Hurrah!" he exclaimed. "The
awful itchy jumper is no more!"

You shouldn't try and copy Theseus step by
step, of course. Anyway, you'd probably have
trouble finding a monster as hideous as the
Minotaur. Though there is always your big
sister's boyfriend.

Because he was a big hero and all that, Theseus got rid of his itchy jumper the hard way. The advice of *The Grantiques Roadshow* is to do it the easy way, i.e.:

1 Take your dog for a walk in the park.

2 Lie down on the park bench with a decent tape in your personal stereo.

3 Tie a loose stitch in your jumper to the dog's collar.

4 Shout "Rabbits!"

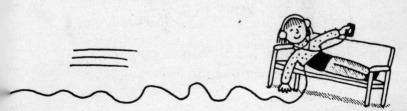

Alternative uses for grans' itchy jumpers: If your dad has a garden, you could offer to sell him your gran's itchy jumper as a scaradactyl. A scaradactyl is like a scarecrow, but much more frightening of course, and is so-called because it can scare a pteradactyl at twenty paces.

Grantique weapon No. 2: Gran-ite Sweets

The second grantique secret weapon to turn up at *The Grantiques Roadshow* was brought along by Neville Greville.

It was an airtight plastic bag. I opened it carefully. And compiled the following facts on its contents . . .

The *Grantiques Roadshow*
Grantique Weapons Factsheet No. 2

GRAN-ITE SWEETS

Designed to act on: Your sense of taste.

What your gran says when you're eating one: "I hope it won't spoil your tea."

What you say when you're eating one: "Umphmubblelobberumubble!"

Tastes like you're eating: Brighton rock (i.e. the one you can see under the end of the pier when the tide's out).

Most resembles: A 3-piece suite.

3-piece suite   Gran-ite sweet

Though, of course, it's a lot easier to eat your way through a 3-piece suite than a gran-ite sweet.

"Umphmubblelobberumubble!"

. . . said Neville. To which I replied, "Don't be shy, now. Spit it out!"
And he did.

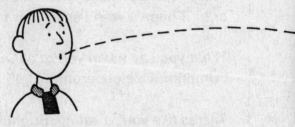

The gran-ite sweet he was sucking, that is.
It whizzed past my left ear and smashed straight through the french windows. Then it bounced off my neighbour Mrs Ram's bottom – oops, I mean my neighbour Mrs Ramsbottom – and landed in the road outside, making a hole as big as a moon crater.

There was no doubt about it. Neville Greville's gran-ite sweet was just like PJ and Duncan's latest release, in other words a *smash hit*.

So rule number one about gran-ite sweets is never, ever spit them out.

"What am I supposed to do with them, then?" asked Neville Greville. "She brings me a whole packet of these things every time she visits!"

Neville Greville had a point.

OUCH!!!

Hmmm . . . and a very sharp one at that, too.

I showed him *The Grantiques Roadshow Gran-ite Sweet Challenge Cup*.

Then I showed him *The Grantiques Roadshow Gran-ite Sweet Challenge Saucer*.

"You are familiar with Conker Championships, in which the winning conker is the hardest one of all? Well, *The Grantiques Roadshow Gran-ite Sweet Championships* is run on exactly the same basis.

"Every year, the championships are held to see who has got the hardest gran-ite sweet of all. So hang on to yours, test them, taste them, find the hardest ones of all.

"And you never know, next year you could be the winner of *The Grantiques Roadshow Gran-ite Sweet Challenge Cup.*"

Neville's cup   Neville's mug

"Neville Greville: *Grantiques Roadshow*
Gran-ite Sweet Challenge Cup Winner,
1995."

Grantique weapon No. 3: Jack-a-Snories

A few weeks later I was visited at *The Grantiques Roadshow* by Mary Lairy.

She had her gran with her.

Before I could say anything, Mary Lairy had opened her mouth to speak. But before Mary Lairy could say anything, her gran had opened *her* mouth and was talking nineteen to the dozen.

Rabbit-rabbit, natter-natter, blah-blah, prattle-prattle, gossip-gossip, chat-chat...

She was telling us a story. There was only one word for it, but she wouldn't stop talking long enough for me to say what it was. Fortunately, there was only one letter for it as well. It was . . .

ZZZZZZZZZZZZZZ . . .

Mary Lairy's gran went on and on. It was just like digging for water in the desert – in other words, *well boring*. I scribbled down a few facts about this particularly effective grantique weapon before I fell asleep . . .

The *Grantiques Roadshow*
Grantique Weapons Factsheet
No. 3

JACK-A-SNORIES

Rabbit-rabbit, natter-natter, etc, etc.

Designed to act on: Your sense of hearing.

What your gran says when she's telling you one: She never tells you just *one*. There are always at least three.

What your gran says when she's telling you at least three: "Now when I was your age . . ." (and so on for about five and a half hours).

What you say when you're listening to one: Snore. Snore.

Feels like: You're being bored to sleep.

What's really happening: You're being bored to sleep.

Mary Lairy asked me:

"How can I stop my gran boring me silly with her stories about the good old days?"

To which I replied, "Zzzzzzzzz . . ."

Then it hit me! The cold flannel Mary Lairy slapped round my face, that is.

Ooooooooooooo!!!!! Brrrrrrrr!!!!!!

"Wake up," said Mary.

So I did. "If you want to stop your gran telling jack-a-snories," I said, "just pop one of these into her mouth every couple of hours."

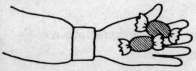

"What are they?" . . . asked Mary Lairy.

"Gran-ite Sweets!" I said.

"Umphmublebobberumubble!"

. . . said Mary Lairy's gran.

Which was a great improvement on, "Now, when I was your age . . .".

Grantique Weapon No. 4: The Photo-greeph

Pete Bogg was the next visitor to *The Grantiques Roadshow*. He seemed very nervous. He was hiding behind a pair of shades.

"I am in despair."

. . . he began. Which didn't tell me a lot. "In despair what? In despair room? Or in despair of well-smart designer jeans?

He looked very uncomfortable. I thought at first this was because his well-smart designer jeans were two sizes too small for him. Then I asked him what it was he had brought along to *The Grantiques Roadshow*.

"Promise you won't laugh?" said Pete Bogg. I said, "Cross my heart and hope to be boiled alive in a vat of lumpy gravy."

Pete Bogg looked around. Then he slowly

pulled out a brown envelope from his pocket
and handed it to me.

I opened it.

No wonder Pete looked as if he wanted
somewhere to hide. What was inside the
envelope was so dreadful, there was nothing
I could say. So I laughed instead.

"Hee-he, ha-ha . . .!"

"You promised you
wouldn't laugh!"
said Pete Bogg.

"Had my fingers crossed. So
there," I replied. What had made
me laugh was this:

"You've got to do something!" . . . sobbed
Pete. So I did. I wrote these notes:

The *Grantiques Roadshow* Grantique Weapons Factsheet No. 4

THE PHOTO-GREEPH

Designed to act on: Your sense of sight.

So-called because: It's a photo and it causes you major greeph.

What it consists of (at best): A photo of you, aged one and a half, wearing only a nappy.

What it consists of (at worst): A photo of you, aged one and a half, not wearing a nappy.

What your gran says when she's showing it to your friends: Aaaahhhhhh…

What you say when your gran's showing it to your friends: Aaaarrrggghhhhhh…!!!!

What your friends say when your gran's showing it to them: Nothing. They're all too busy rolling around the floor laughing.

There is a very good way of getting rid of photo-greephs. It goes like this.

YOU: That's a really great photo-greeph, Gran!
GRAN: It is, isn't it!
YOU: Why don't you get it enlarged?

"What! That's a stupid idea!" exclaimed Pete Bogg.

"Be quiet and let me finish the story," I said.
GRAN: I think I will get it enlarged, you know.
You steer your gran in the direction of CheapSnaps, the cut-price photo shop. (It's next to CheapSkates, the cut-price roller-blade shop.) Make sure you get served by Ed (known to all as Thick Ed). Say to him:
YOU: Hello, Ed. My gran would like this photo blown up, please.
THICK ED: Right you are.

Whereupon Ed places a small bomb under it.

Result: The chances are your photo-greeph will end up as a pile of tiny fragments, but it's probably best if you and your gran don't hang around to check this.

Grantiques weapon No. 5: Stinky Soap

Hannah Spanner was my last visitor. "Over here, boys!"

. . . she yelled, as a beefy lorry driver and his mate lowered a reinforced safe through the ceiling with a crane. All the *Grantiques Roadshow* experts dived for cover.

Unfortunately, *The Grantiques Roadshow* wasn't being held in a pool, but a Pool Hall.

Everyone was very angry indeed. "You seem to have created quite a stink," I said to Hannah Spanner.

"Not half as much a stink as there is in there!" she replied, pointing to the safe. I undid the fifty-three locks. Then I undid the sixty-three bolts.

Quickly I shut the door again. I knew exactly what it was that Hannah Spanner had brought along:

The *Grantiques Roadshow* Grantique Weapons Factsheet No. 5

STINKY SOAP

Designed to act on: Your sense of smell.

So-called because: It's soap and it stinks.

What your gran thinks it's for:
1. Washing your face. 2. And behind your ears.

What it's really for: 1. Clearing blocked drains. 2. Clearing crowded rooms.

Where your gran thinks it should go: Behind your ears – and properly this time!

Where you know *it goes:* Right up your nose.

There's only one way to deal with Stinky Soap and that's with a beetroot. All you need to do is follow these simple steps:

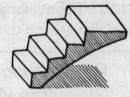

Now follow these rather more complicated steps:

Grantiques Roadshow
Factsheet

SIMPLE STEPS FOR GETTING RID OF STINKY SOAP

1 Cut a beetroot in half.
2 Rub the juicy side on the underneath of your gran's bar of Stinky Soap.
3 At bath-time, rub the beetroot-y side of the soap behind your ears.
4 You now look as if you've just been served as the main course at a vampire's dinner party.
5 Yell for your gran. She will come running – take a horrified glance at your neck and –

This is what will happen next:

YOU: Granny! Dear Granny! Whatever you do, don't touch the Stinky Soap, I beg of you!
GRAN: Why, dear child, whatever is it?
YOU: (*Clasping your neck. Faintly*) Stinkysoaposis!

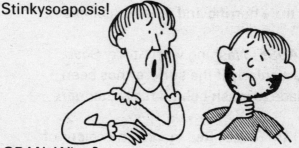

GRAN: What?
YOU: Stinkysoaposis! Haven't you read about it?

(*At this point, you thrust a scrap of paper in her hand. It is, in fact, page 84 of this book.*)

GRAN: (*Looking at the paper*) I can't make head or tail of it.
YOU: Why not?
GRAN: I haven't got my reading glasses on!

(*At this point, you fetch your gran her reading glasses.*)

GRAN: Thank you, dear.

Dr Crippen's Dictionary of Really Hideous and Horrible Diseases

STINKYSOAPOSIS

A truly horrific and hideous complaint.

CAUSE: Washing with Stinky Soap. Particularly if the sufferer has been made to wash behind his or her ears.

SYMPTOMS: Red marks, the colour of beetroot. After a bit, the patient's ears will drop off and eventually, after months of painful agony, the patient's head will drop off.

One week   One month   Six months

Particularly susceptible to Stinkysoaposis are grandchildren.

CURE: None whatsoever.

No sooner has your gran finished reading this than she will pick up the Stinky Soap with her coal tongs and bury it deep in the back garden, where its repulsive smell will kill off any slugs in her vegetable patch.

TEST YOURSELF!!! on grantique weapons

Find the five grantique weapons in this gran's house. Then circle them and draw a line from them to the right label.

Itchy Jumper   Jack-a-Snories

Gran-ite Sweets

The Photo-greeph   The Stinky Soap

TEST YOURSELF AGAIN!!! on grantique weapons

Match the following grantique weapons to the word that best describes them:

GRANTIQUE WEAPONS

WORDS THAT DESCRIBE THEM

1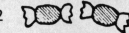

a   (ZZZZZZZ!)

2

b   (EE·OW OUCH!)

3

c   (UMPHMUBBLE LOBBERUMUBBLE!)

4

d   (POOH!)

5

e   (AAAARGH!)

Answers 1 = b; 2 = c; 3 = a; 4 = e; 5 = d.

How To Handle Your Gran: Stage Five

Eight very important facts you should know about grans

1 What's the name of the TV programme about a whole lot of grans who live in a forest?
Answer: The Granny-mals of Farthing Wood.

2 What do you call the knobbly bits half-way up a gran's legs?
Answer: Gran-knees.

3 What do you call a sheep's granny?
Answer: A baa-nana.

4 What do you call forty grannies jumping over a hedge?
Answer: The Gran National.

5 What do you call a nan with a blue light on her head?
Answer: A Pa-nan-da car.

6 What do you call a granny in a sentry box?
Answer: A Granadier Guard.

7 What do you get if you sit a granny on a chicken?
Answer: Granbled eggs.

8 What do you call a gran with six tons of high explosive in her handbag?
Answer: Dy-nana-mite.

How To Handle Your Gran: Stage Six

The *Grantiques Roadshow* all-purpose gran letters

All grans like getting letters. Experts from *The Grantiques Roadshow* have devised these all-purpose letters which you can use to send to your gran. Just cross out the words you don't need!

Dear { Gran / Nan / Nana

Thank you for the { Itchy Jumper / Gran-ite Sweets / mountain bike / pony

which you { welded / chiselled / will send } me for { Christmas. / my birthday. / next Christmas.

I shall look forward very much to { unravelling it. / riding it. / dropping it on Mum's foot

I hope your { leg / TV / other leg } isn't playing up too much.

Love to { Grandad. / Tiddles the cat. / Alan the goldfish.

Lots of love,

Dear { Gran
       Nan
       Nana

Thank you very much for having me to stay.

I had a wonderful { time.
                    journey home.
                    sleep.

I am glad to say that the doctors say I should

make a full recovery from { Stinkysoaposis.
                            my prunes and bran overdose.
                            being bored into a 7-day coma
                               by your jack-a-snories.

I hope your { leg
              TV   Isn't playing up too much.
              other leg

Love to { Grandad.
          Tiddles the cat.
          Alan the goldfish.

Lots of love,

How To Handle Your Gran: Stage Seven

Compiling your very own gran file

Why it is important to keep a file on your gran*

It's very easy to forget all the facts about the type of gran you have got. Unless you are an elephant of course: then it's very easy to *remember* everything about the type of gran you have got, because elephants *never* forget.

That's right.

What sort of files you can keep on your gran

There are three sorts of files you could keep on your gran.

* Or grans, if you've got two.

AN OPEN FILE   A NAIL FILE

A SECRET FILE: I can't show you what a secret file looks like. ('Cos it's secret.)

How do I keep a file on my gran?

Stick it on tightly with Sellotape – or fill in the questionnaire on the next page. Use the file to fill in details about both your grans, if you have two.

How do I make sure my gran doesn't see my file on her?

Either (i) hide it somewhere she'd never want to look, e.g. inside one of your oldest and smelliest trainers; or (ii) hide her reading glasses.

GRAN FILE

MY NAME ....

MY GRAN'S NAME ....

MY GRAN'S AGE	Old/Really Old	Old/Really Old
	Ancient/	Ancient
	Prehistoric	Prehistoric
EYES	Blue/Green	Blue/Green
	Brown/Beady	Brown/Beady
HAIR	White/Black/	White/Black
	Blonde/Brown	Blonde/Brown
	Blue/Green/	Blue/Green
	Violet/Pink*	Violet/Pink*
	Orange with	Orange with
	mauve stripes**	mauve stripes**

THE GOOD NEWS ABOUT YOUR GRAN

Is she good at telling really wicked stories about
how naughty Mum/Dad were when they were
my age?   YES/NO   YES/NO

Can she cook really scrummy
meals?   YES/NO   YES/NO

Does she take me to really ace
places?   YES/NO   YES/NO

Does she like giving me lots of pocket
money?   YES/NO   YES/NO

*You've got a pink gran   **You've got a punk gran.*

THE BAD NEWS ABOUT YOUR GRAN

Is she a telly-gran?	YES/NO	YES/NO
Is she a bran gran?	YES/NO	YES/NO
Is she a kisser-gran?	YES/NO	YES/NO
Is she a grow-nan?	YES/NO	YES/NO

WHICH OF THE FOLLOWING SECRET GRANTIQUE WEAPONS DOES SHE USE?

The Itchy Jumper?	YES/NO	YES/NO
Gran-ite Sweets?	YES/NO	YES/NO
Jack-a-Snories?	YES/NO	YES/NO
The Photo-greeph?	YES/NO	YES/NO
Stinky Soap?	YES/NO	YES/NO

How it all ended – another letter from my gran

Flat 80 The Old Granary
75 Gran Parade
Nantwich
NA1 NA2

My dear grandson

Happy birthday.

A few months ago I wrote to tell you that if you ever wrote a book about how to handle your gran, I would never, ever send you a maroon zip-up cardigan again.

I hear that you have written a book about how to handle your gran.

Now I may be an old fuddy-duddy, but I am a woman of my word. I am _not_ sending you any more maroon zip-up cardigans.

Enclosed instead, is a dark green button-up cardigan.

Your ever doting
Gran

P.S. NOT YOUR OTHER GRAN